# ONE HELLUVA MOVE

## Don't Settle For Safe

## MARK JOHNSON

◁◆▷

# ENDORSEMENTS

Mark provides a blueprint full of important information for those of you who want to create a better more predicable business. - **Steve Murray, CEO and Founder of REAL TRENDS, the Trusted Source of news, analysis, and information on the residential brokerage industry since 1987.**

You'll find nuggets of gold inside this fast reading, quick summary of success. In my business I've discovered our traction, our rocket fuel and how to get a grip. Inside these pages find something you can execute and take action on today! – **Gabe Abshire, CEO and Founder of Utility Concierge**

In this snapshot of successful practices, Mark delivers a must read for anyone looking to create more success. **Nicole Espinosa, Author, Team Leader and Short Sale Expert.**

A quick practical guide to success, Mark takes you through a series of steps designed to get you out of your head and intro action. - **JP Piccinini, CEO and Founder of JP & Associates REALTORS®.**

# DEDICATION

This series is dedicated to my sons – Stephen, Timothy and Andrew - who I have seen grow into amazing young men. And, to the my many mentors along the way – Larry Perkins, Bill Peterson, Jon Cook, Neil Shusterman, Martin Dugard and many others who taught me that love and profit can go hand in hand.

**Consider This:**
One of my favorite passages to read several times each year as written by Price Pritchett, PH.D. in his book "You2 - A High Velocity Formula for Multiplying Your Personal Effectiveness:"

Right now, in this moment, you are capable of exponential improvement in your performance. You can multiple your personal effectiveness, hit new highs, and shatter old records. The results you can have will be hard for you to imagine.

**You can become you squared.**

You do not have to settle for things as they are right now. That can change. If you are ready, life is prepared to give you a breakthrough.

You do not have to be content with improving things incrementally or gradually. Just as your level of performance can improve drastically, so can your rate of accomplishment,

Face it, you have not been reaching your full potential, so far, you have not even come close. No matter how you wish to measure success, regardless of how you define achievement, you have barely scratched the surface. But maybe the time has come to change all that. Maybe you are ready for a quantum leap.

# FORWARD

It only takes one decision to move from fear to faith. With that one step, others just like you have moved from doubt to
certainty and from indifference to significance. A common theme among all top performers – executives, sales professionals, athletes, celebrities and those who make an impact, is knowing how to get there.

Success I've found is simply making a decision to believe when no one else believes. This book is about building a life and business around the goals you have set out to achieve, surrounding yourself with winners and discipline yourself to execute even on the days when no one believes in you but yourself. To stay the course when things get hard  and there is no one to talk to, when the struggles become real and the addictions need to be broken.

Success isn't built with will-power, it is built by aligning your behaviors with your goals. Inside these pages you'll find a blueprint, short stories, tools and resources to help you achieve your success.

Mark Johnson shares his decades of experience in helping, honing and honoring those on the journey of creating a business and life by design. Mark believes in the power to say no... to believe ... to work ... to fail and to succeed. You are someone who has been given power beyond your current beliefs to achieve whatever you have decided to do, and it is nothing more than these very beliefs that WILL allow you to make it!

# TABLE OF CONTENTS

# BONUS SECTION

# ATTITUDE TRUMPS SKILLS

**"Leadership is practiced not so much in words as in attitude and in actions."** - Harold S. Geneen

Harold Gennen understood that skill is necessary, yet attitude is a differentiator. As CEO of the International Telephone and Telegraph Corporation (ITT) he grew the company from a medium-sized business with $765 million sales in 1961, into an international conglomerate with $17 billion in sales by 1970. That type of growth does not happen by chance. It happens by design. Harold knew then what many CEO's like Mary Barra of General Motors; Marc Benioff of Salesforce; Jeff Bezos of Amazon and Warren Buffet of Berkshire-Hathaway know now: Attitude Trumps Skills... Every Day!

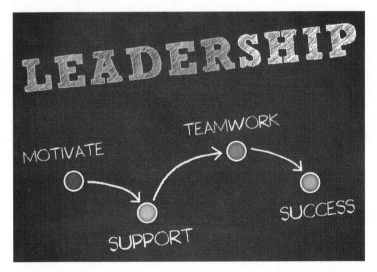

My first college degree provided me with a highly desirable and marketable skill, at a time when the economy was in terrible condition. And, while I decided to serve full time as a US Army officer, my perspective was that the skills I had obtained in college and in officer training would be the key driver for my future career success. I was wrong...

1

As a young Lieutenant, I quickly learned that skills were important, yet they evolve so quickly. The equipment you have today is replaced by new equipment tomorrow. Skills of today quickly became outdated and new skills are required. I have found the key to being more effective is driven by adopting a perspective of life-long learning and the attitudinal attributes of collaboration, communication and project leadership.

Why does attitude matter? Bloomberg indicates eight out of ten businesses fail in the first eighteen months. A study by Leadership IQ also found nearly 46% of hires into positions fail within eighteen months. Why? The number one reason sighted by their leaders was "poor interpersonal skills that were overlooked in the startup, on- boarding or hiring process."

So, whether you are a hiring manager, a team leader or a solo entrepreneur here are some of the critical focal points for you and your team to be mindful of:

Attitudes of **Entitlement** can show up us as a symptom of poor work ethic.

Attitudes of **Indifference** might explain why goals and deadlines are consistently missed.

Attitudes that are **Pretentious** could explain unnecessary stress and strain within a team or a family.

Attitudes of **Coach-ability**. As a leader it is important to provide a growth mindset allowing you to be open to feedback and constructive criticism because statistics show 26% of the false starts in business can be attributed to a fixed mindset whereby you reject any type of coaching or constructive feedback.

Attitudes of **Emotional Intelligence**. Understanding and having command of your own emotions and the ability to read and react to others, emotions are critical to success today. Yet regardless of the skill base, 23% of false starts in business occur because of poor emotional intelligence.

Attitudes of **Inspiration**. Inspiration is something you feel on the inside, motivation is something from the outside that compels you to take action. You might have the most amazing skills on the planet, yet ultimately fail because you simply lack ambition, the inspiration that gets you up and running every day.

Attitudes of **Gratitude** can remove barriers, inspire trust and build loyalty.

Attitudes of **Humility and Service** can promote genuine customer appreciation and outstanding customer service.

Jerry's story is worth repeating, it's cited and used frequently yet still so powerful. Jerry was a restaurant manager. He was always in a good mood and always had something positive to say. When someone would ask him how he was doing, he would reply "if I were any better I'd be twins!"

3

Jerry was offered a managerial job at another restaurant and many of the wait staff and customers followed him. When asked why; they responded, because of his attitude... Jerry is a natural motivator, his attitude is contagious. When asked what the secret to his positive attitude is, Jerry indicated it was a matter of choice. Each morning he said, I have two choices: I can choose to be in a good mood and be positive to others or I can choose to be in a bad mood and be negative towards others. If someone is complaining, I can choose to accept the complaint, or I can learn from it and find the positive in it.

What makes Jerry's story even more powerful is this; his restaurant was robbed at gun point and he was shot with life threatening wounds! Despite these life-threatening injuries, Jerry made the doctors and nurses laugh and he later fully recovered. When asked about how this impacted him, Jerry talked about choices. I could choose to be a victim, or I can choose to move forward towards my dreams.

At this point your self talking is saying, "Mark... it is just not that easy!" Yet, Jerry would say, "Yes, it is!" Business and life is all about choices. Every situation is a choice. You choose how you react to every situation. You choose how other people affect your mood. Jerry made his choice and you make yours.

Here is what I know, many of you reading this are self-employed entrepreneurs. Life will get in the way of your business. At that moment, you cannot change the circumstances, you can only make the choices to continue ensuring your income stream is protected. Like Jerry, you owe it to yourself, to your staff, customers, family and loved ones to remain mentally tough.

During a particularly harder time in my life, one of my coaches taught me a definition of mental toughness and

**4**

attitude that Jerry would embrace and has served me well too:

**"Mental toughness is the choice - the attitude - of staying in inspired action despite the circumstances surrounding you."**

I am not suggesting we ignore life's challenges. For most of us reading this right now we simply do not have the luxury of giving up. Having an attitude of perseverance and making the decision to stay in positive action despite the circumstances surrounding us is a choice that serves well.

The Leadership IQ study found the most successful people differentiated themselves by having a strong focus on the attitudinal factors like coach-ability, emotional intelligence, ambition and positive temperament.

Unlike skills, attitudes are a choice. Viktor Frankl said it so well:

**"Everything can be taken away from you but one thing: The last of human freedoms – to choose one's attitude in any given set of circumstances, is to choose one's own way."**

Are you going to continue to settle for safe or make One Helluva Move? Some practical steps to make "One Helluva Move" this week:

**For Yourself:**

Reflect on those you most admire and consider who has impacted you most favorably. List them by name. I will bet when you reflect on this list it is the attitude traits not the skills that make these people stand out.

5

What practical steps can you apply in your approach to relationships and in business this week?

**For Building Your Team:**

Reflect on your hiring practices. Who are your peak performers? What makes them stand out? I will bet you it is the attitudinal factors we have discussed. Skill is necessary, yet attitudes are the differentiator of peak performers. Consider the process outlined in the bonus section to bring your interview strategy to the next level of effectiveness.

What steps can you take to improve your team dynamics this week?

# Bonus Section:
# Interview Questions To Determine Attitude

**This Interview Strategy Will Allow You To:**
Discover their habits
Discover their history
Discover their ambitions
Discover their beliefs
Discover their emotional intelligence
Minimize asking what is on the resume

**Power Questions That Uncover Attitudes:**
What do you do?
How did you get started? Where are your originally from?
What else do you do besides work?
Who has had the biggest impact on you? What did that person teach you?
As you look at business as a radarscope there are highs and lows...
What is a low point? What is a high point?
What does that tell you about yourself? What got you through the lows?
If someone asked you for advice on how to run a business what would you tell them?
What does the future hold for you?
When your career is over, how do you want to be remembered?
In addition, you will want to ask 1, 2 or 3 skills-based questions related to the given assignment.

# THE WHEEL OF LIFE
# IS YOUR TIRE FLAT?

▼

**"I made my own assessment of my life, and I began to live it. That was freedom."** - Fernando Flores

We often hear stories of outsiders who seem to come from nowhere to achieve success. In looking at these success stories, the starting point for the breakthrough always comes from a gap analysis.

Either from desperation or inspiration, something triggers the need to re-asses what is working and what is not working in your life or in your career.

A speaker was encouraging her audience to get out of their comfort zones and not settle for safe. After the talk, a woman wrote her and stated she would never drive 200 miles to the big city alone. She would wait for her husband or a friend to drive her there. She lived in fear... what if the car broke down, what if I get lost? Yet, the woman in this story was inspired to initiate change because she was tired of living in fear. She was tired of waiting for others, so she got in her car drove to the big city. She got a little lost yet said in her letter, "I found the shopping mall, got  back home and now I feel so good about myself!"

She learned how empowering and positive change can be. She was no longer bound by her fears. She could drive with someone, or she could go alone. She developed courage, found freedom, and built her self-esteem.

**She changed because she was inspired to change.**

No matter how accomplished or joyful we are, we all have areas of our life that could use some improvement. Think about it... does your job feel like a job, something you go to every day to earn income, or does it feel like a mission, something you would do even if you were not paid for it? What about your relationships? Are the relationships you care about the most as fulfilling and satisfying as you desire?

The Wheel of Life is one way to take a look at each facet of life, and rate its relative quality level, so you can uncover which areas need more attention than others. Consider each area like a spoke of a wheel: when all of the spokes are aligned you have a smooth ride! Yet when one or more of the spokes is uneven than the others, your wheel is off balance and you have a bumpy ride.

Once you understand the gaps in each of your critical areas of focus on the wheel of life you can begin to close them and create breakthroughs.

With this exercise, you can identify where you are excelling and where there is room for improvement.

**Directions:** The seven sections in the Wheel of Life represent different aspects of your life. Seeing the center of the wheel as 1 and the outer edges as 10, rank your level of satisfaction with each life area. The new perimeter represents the wheel of your life. If this were a real wheel, how bumpy would your ride be? Complete the wheel for where you were 2 years ago; today and where you want to be next year:

## 2 Years Ago

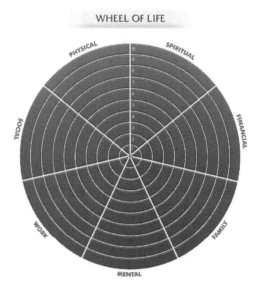

## Today

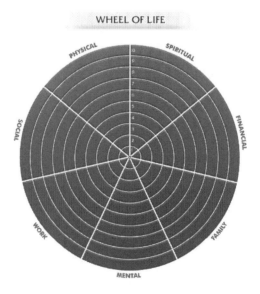

## Next Year

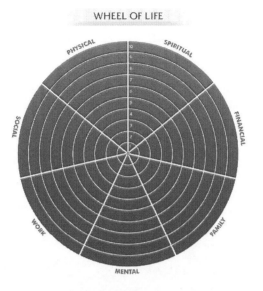

WHEEL OF LIFE

PHYSICAL    SPIRITUAL

SOCIAL    FINANCIAL

WORK    FAMILY

MENTAL

As a business coach and from my personal experience, I would remind you this exercise is not about achieving a perfect 10... it is about creating a smooth ride.

I would ask you:

- How much progress have you made from 2 years ago?
- What area would you like to work on the most now?
- Which area are you willing to make a change in now?
- How will your wheel look a year from today?
- Who do you need to BE to make that happen?

Most of my clients hire me for real estate business coaching so they naturally gravitate towards work and career. So, let's peel the onion back one additional layer.

We know that attitude trumps skills every day, yet even with a great attitude there are some basic skills required to achieve your goals. Those skills might include your ability to communicate and to influence others. The question is: What are your abilities? In sales, if you lack the knowledge of what to say or basic selling skills, you will consistently struggle. Let's uncover the gaps in your skills.

**Directions:** The 8 sections in the Circle of Skills represent different aspects of your sales career. And, regardless if you are in sales or not, in some aspect we are all salespeople. Seeing the center of the wheel as 1 and the outer edges as 10, rank your level of satisfaction with each skill area. The new perimeter represents the circle of skills. Like the wheel of life, if this were a real wheel, how bumpy would your ride be? Complete the wheel for where you were now and where you want to be at the end of 90 days and 6 months and 1 year from now.

You can take this example and translate it to whatever specific skills apply your profession. This one works for someone in real estate sales.

## My Current State

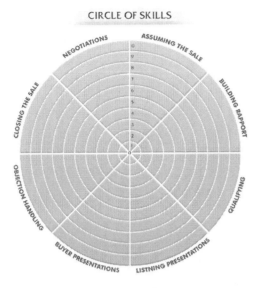

## 90 days from now

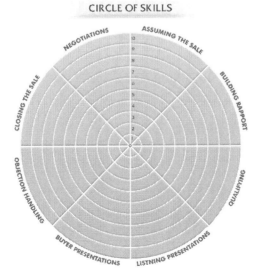

## 6 Months from Now

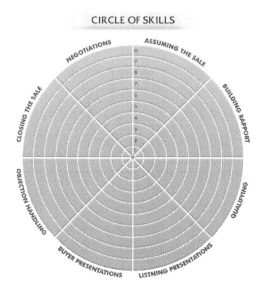

## One Year From Now

Wow that's a lot, are you overwhelmed?

If so, that is natural, and it is ok. Anytime you do a comprehensive assessment it is natural to say, "I have so much work to do!" Yet here is what I know: when you back up and look at this from a big picture perspective and break it down into smaller chunks it becomes very manageable.

As a coach, and from my personal experience I would remind you now just like the Wheel of Life this exercise is not about achieving a perfect 10, it is about creating a smooth ride. I would ask you... "What area would you like to work on the most or which area are you ready and willing to make a change in now?

Most of us can only focus on one or two major goals at a time. So, the key is a plan... a plan for the next 30 days, 60 days and 90 days or more. You have a choice to make today, a choice to change your approach or settle for the status quo.

The extraordinary people I have known take action. They are willing to step out in action and possibly make a mistake because they know even if they fail, they will learn a lesson and move onward and upward.

You might be asking yourself, what if I make a mistake, what if I fail? The extraordinary people I have known have learned to change their definition of a mistake. Think about it...it is not the mistake itself but the conversation you have in your head about what the mistake means. Face it, you are going to make mistakes. So, when you do make a mistake rather than beat yourself up over it, declare it perfect.

When you declare a mistake, a mistake... you are left with more of the same and a feeling of defeat. When you declare it perfect, document your learnings and move forward you have power. I choose to have the power!

**"Mistakes are the portals of discovery."**

Let's explore the importance of a plan with the tale of two sales people. Both enter their fields with aspirations or freedom, money and control of their destiny. They both interview and join the same company, they take the same training, work in the same office and compete in the same marketplace; essentially, they start out their careers in with equal possibilities and opportunities.

Fast forward five years... one is wildly successful and the other is out of the business. What is the difference between the two? The PLAN. One of them figured out if they were to write down their goals, create a strategy, execute of a series of action plans and systems and follow a basic schedule, s/he ultimately would achieve the dream.

The tale of these two salespeople is simple. One became a planner and worked a plan every day to become successful. S/he knew their daily number to achieve, their goals and created daily action plans. The other one started the day hoping and praying to do a little more, to do a little better today yet, had no specific plan or specific strategy. He simply threw his dreams up to luck and chance... to the whim of the market or whatever showed up in the office that day.

The single most important distinction of those I have seen achieve success is a specific and actionable plan, executed with discipline.

The lesson: Develop a plan and create a strategy for yourself that will allow you to achieve all you desire. And be very clear. Specific detailed plans get rewarded while vague plans get punished. Declare it perfect and keep these three principles in mind about the three decisions we control:

You control what you choose to focus on.

You control the meaning you attach to things (events, communications, interactions).

You control what to do in spite of the obstacles thrown front of you

Are you going to continue to settle for safe or make One Helluva Move? Some practical steps to make "One Helluva Move" this week:

**For Yourself:**

What ONE area from the Wheel of Life are you committed to taking action on in the next 30 days? What mistakes do you need to declare "perfect?"

_____
_____
_____
_____
_____
_____

What ONE area from the Circle of Skills are you committed to taking action on in the next 30 days? What mistakes do you need to declare "perfect?"

_____
_____
_____
_____
_____
_____

Who will be your accountability partner in the actions listed above?

      1. _____

      2. _____


Write a letter to your future self, dated one year from today and give it to your accountability partner to hand to you six months from now!

**For Building Your Team:**

What is possible with your team, when you take them through the wheel of life and circle of skills exercise? What ONE area would increase the effectiveness of your team?

_____
_____
_____
_____
_____


As the team leader, your job is to make sure your team members reach their goals... How can you better support your team in achieving all of their goals?

_____
_____
_____
_____
_____


Bonus Assignment – Basics of a Plan and Possible Strategies

Why should someone work with me or my firm?

      1. _____

      2. _____

      3. _____

What do I love about my profession?

        1. _____
        2. _____
        3. _____

How many sales would I like to make in the next twelve months?

How many appointments do I need to make one sale?

How many conversations do I need to make one appointment?

What actions do I need to take to create the necessary number of conversations?

What are my daily numbers - for each work day - from each of the above?

How can I use, convert all the items listed above into a business strategy that works for me?

# DESIRE, DECISIONS, DETERMINATION AND DISCIPLINE ... THE ART & SCIENCE OF GOAL SETTING

---

**"Setting goals is the first step in turning the invisible into the visible."** - Tony Robbins

Price Pritchett, the author of "You2" wrote it best, "You don't have to know how you're going to get there, but you do need to know where you want to go!" There is magic in operating with a sharply defined mental image of the outcome you seek. Visualize your arrival. When you do that, it Is like a magnet to the ways and means and the methods to get there. The solutions begin to appear, and the answers come to you.

## Desire

A young man asked Socrates the secret to success. Socrates told the young man to meet near the river the next morning.

The next morning, they met. Socrates asked the young man to walk with him toward the river. When the water got up to their neck, Socrates took the young man by surprise and ducked him into the water. The boy struggled to get out, yet Socrates was strong and kept him there until the boy started turning blue. Socrates pulled his head out of the water and the first thing the young man did was to  gasp and take a deep breath of air.

Socrates asked, 'What did you want the most when you were there?" The boy replied, "Air." Socrates said:

**"That is the secret to success. When you want success as badly as you wanted the air, then you will get it." There is no other secret.**

Just like a small fire cannot give much heat, a weak desire cannot produce great results... a burning desire is the starting point of all accomplishment. If you truly want to achieve your stated goal, the first step is desire. You must want it badly enough to make an unshakable commitment and to be willing to make sacrifices.

## Decision

I have found from my own experience that I was getting in my own way. Can you relate? You know the doubts, anxieties, ego, fear and those never ending critical inner voices. The very things that keep us from taking action. And not taking action is a decision in and of itself, yes?

And thus, the second D is Decision. Getting out of my own way meant becoming more self-aware of those thoughts that held me back and the courage and mental toughness to step forward.

Sometime ago, I was worried whether or not I should take on a new assignment. By that time, I was learning how I could get out of my own way, so I stopped for a moment of reflection and gratitude. That time allowed me to be curious rather than being consumed by fear and worry. I reflected on the meaning I was attaching to things associated with this new assignment. This allowed me to shift my thoughts away from the distractions and simply be present and aware. By doing so I was free to find clarity and to make a more rational decision about this new assignment. Fear and worry became optional for me and the clarity to make a decision and move forward powerfully became easier.

Are you ready, right now, to make a decision to do whatever is necessary, to be willing to pay any price, go any distance, to achieve your goal?

## Determination

The third D, Determination is demonstrated by Richard Branson who has dyslexia, Walt Disney who pitched nearly 300 possible investors before anyone took interest, Bill Gates' whose first business failed; Albert Einstein who did not speak until he was four, Jim Carrey who was homeless, and Stephen King whose first novel was rejected 30 times.

So, what is greater in your life right now...excuses as to why you are not achieving as much as you want to, or mega doses of determination to get what you want? I have learned that determination is a function of three factors: a **goal**; a **commitment** and a **focus**.

## Goals

Goals are like magnets that attract us to a higher ground and new horizons. They give our eyes a focus, our mind an aim, and our strength a purpose. Without their pull, we would remain forever stationary, incapable of moving forward.

A goal is a possibility that fulfills a dream.

You know the importance of setting goals ... so why is it so hard to keep and reach them? We have all felt the excitement that comes with setting a new goal, but then, as time progresses, excitement can morph into anxiety. This is because we are facing the reality that we are so far from our goal and have no framework or strategy of how to get there. Let's start with the three types of goals:

## Outcome Goals

An outcome goal is one that is not really under your control. Instead, it is based on outside circumstances. For example, if your goal is to the #1 selling agent in your market, that is a goal that is not only based on your numbers, but also the numbers from other agents in your market too.

## Performance Goals

Performance goals are personal achievement goals. They are the building blocks that help you reach your outcome goal. A good performance goal example is to "beat my personal record of 21 homes sold in a year."

## Process Goals

Process goals are completely under your control and are composed of the things you do on a daily basis like habits and routines. Think of these as the small steps you take to get to your performance and outcome goals every single day. An example of a process goal would be to "spend 90 minutes prospecting daily" or "call 30 FSBO's every Monday."

In over 650 studies completed with over 50,000 participants, scientists analyzed what worked best when goal setting. Overall, individuals who focused on Process Goals had more success in reaching their goals than those who simply set Performance or Outcome Goals.

In addition, it was observed that specific and challenging goals are far more effective than vague goals of "trying to do your best" goals. This is where **S.M.A.R.T.** goals come into play.

**S.M.A.R.T.** is an acronym that you can use to guide your goal setting. To make sure your goals are clear and reachable, each one should be:

S - specific - (simple, sensible, significant)
M - measurable - (meaningful, motivating)
A - achievable - (attainable and realistic)
R - relevant - (realistic & resourced, results based)
T - time Bound - (timely & time-sensitive)

At the end of this chapter, you'll find one template that might work just for you. Or change it up to fit your needs.

**Commitment**

The Scottish mountaineer, William Hutchison Murray, wrote about commitment in his book, "The Scottish Himalayan Expedition." He wrote: "Until one is committed there is hesitancy...the moment one definitely commits oneself, then providence moves too. All sorts of things occur to help one that would never otherwise have occurred."

**Focus**

Dr. Allen Zimmerman, wrote about focus this way. It is simply another way of saying you have got to keep your eye on the goal.

One of three boys learned just that. As they were playing in the deep snow, a neighbor asked them if they wanted to have a race. He said he would give a prize to the winner.

It sounded good to the boys, so they gathered around the man to learn more. He told them the winner would not be the one who ran the fastest but the one who ran the straightest line. He said he would go to the other end of the field, give a signal, and have them race to him.

The boys took off. The first one looked at his feet as he ran to make sure they were pointing straight ahead. The second boy wondered how straight the boys on either side of him were running and tried to line himself up with them. The third boy just kept his eyes fixed on the man at the end of the field. He kept his eyes fixed on the goal. And, of course, he won the race. His line was by far the straightest.

The two losers lost their focus. They got distracted from the goal. In fact, they made the two most common mistakes people make when trying to achieve their goals.

The first boy became self-conscious. He spent too much time worrying about the possible mistakes he was making.

The second boy spent too much time wondering how his competitors were doing.

Do not make those mistakes. You will not only lose the race, but you' will also lose your determination for other races in life.

You can have DETERMINATION. You can be as successful as you want — as long as you avoid the excuses and stay focused on the outcome.

### Discipline

The fourth D is something we all can relate to. You know the time you know what you want to do, yet you derail yourself with unaligned behaviors?

Understanding the science of Discipline can help. For starters, without a strong desire to achieve a specific goal there is little hope for discipline. Think about... write down a goal you have failed to achieve. Now right down a goal that you nailed. For each of these scenarios reflect on:

What you wanted?

Why you wanted it?

What specifically you did or did not do to achieve the goal(s)?

Did you mentally rehearse the actions you needed to take to make it happen?

After reflecting on those scenarios what patterns or behaviors did you identify? What distinctions did you identify for the goal you achieved vs. the one you missed? Typically, those that succeed in goal achievement follow a pattern. A pattern of having a compelling reason **why** they want to accomplish the goal; they develop an unwavering **commitment** and **accountability**; they create **rewards and penalties**; they create **personal standards** and they **gamify** or create a competitive environment.

Those that succeed in goal achievement, know that we are what we repeatedly do. Excellence, then, is not an act, but a habit. In "The Power of Habit", Charles Duhigg delivers a framework for understanding how habits work and a guide to experimenting with how they might change. That framework is:

Triggers: the event that starts the routine

Routines: the behavior you perform

Rewards: the benefit that is associated with the behavior

Once we understand our triggers, our routines and our rewards we can proactively understand the triggers and switch out poor routines with more empowering routines and thus create disciplined behaviors that are aligned with the goals.

Discipline requires penalties and rewards. Our motivation levels often ebb and flow as we pursue our goal. At certain times you will feel extremely motivated, while at other times you will struggle to get through specific tasks and activities.

To level out these these cycles, it can be helpful to put some penalties and rewards in place. Punishments and awards can be used to help direct your behavior throughout the day.

You can, for instance, reward yourself for making particular choices or for certain kinds of behaviors. Likewise, you can penalize yourself for indulging in other types of behaviors or for making poor choices. These penalties and rewards will add another element to the furnace that will keep the fuel of discipline burning throughout the day. Tony Robbins, the world class life and business choice as plenty of material you can read about to better understand if you are driven towards pleasure (rewards) or away from pain (penalties). It boils down to:

What behaviors and choices will I accept?

What behaviors and choices will I not accept?

How will I correct things when I get off track?

Essentially, this all comes down to making simple agreements with yourself. Agreements about what you will and will not accept are the cornerstone of discipline. It then requires holding yourself accountable for following through with these agreements.

Excuses are like noses. We have all got one and they smell. Are you going to continue to settle for safe or make One Helluva Move? Some practical steps to make "One Helluva Move" this week:

**For Yourself:**

What is it you REALLY want?

_____

_____

_____

_____

Why do you want it?

_____

_____

_____

_____

What specifically do you need to do to get it done?

_____

_____

_____

_____

How can I mentally rehearse the actions I will take to make it happen?

_____

_____

_____

_____

Who will help you maintain accountability to the above?

_____

_____

_____

_____

**For Building Your Team:**

What is it you REALLY want?

_____
_____
_____
_____

Why do you want it?

_____
_____
_____
_____

What specifically do you need to do to get it done?

_____
_____
_____
_____

Are your team members aligned and do they buy into this vision? (If not, what has to happen to get alignment?)

_____
_____
_____
_____

How can you and your team members mentally rehearse the actions needed to make it happen?

_____
_____
_____
_____

Who will help you maintain accountability to the above?

_____
_____
_____

# S.M.A.R.T. Goal Worksheet

Today's Date: _____Target Date:_____
          Start Date: _____

                    Goal:


## Verify that your goal is S.M.A.R.T.

**Specific:** What exactly will you accomplish?

_____
_____
_____
_____
_____


**Measurable:** How will you know when you have reached this goal?

_____
_____
_____
_____
_____


**Achievable:** Is achieving this goal realistic with effort and commitment? Have you got the resources to achieve this goal? If not, how will you get them?

_____
_____
_____
_____
_____

**Relevant:** Why is this goal significant to your life?

_____

_____

_____

_____

_____

_____

**Timely:** When will you achieve this goal?

_____

_____

_____

_____

_____

**This goal is important because:**

_____

_____

_____

_____

_____

_____

**The benefits of achieving this goal will be:**

_____

_____

_____

_____

_____

_____

**Taking Action:**

**Potential Obstacles & Potential Solutions**

_____
_____
_____
_____
_____
_____
_____

**Who are the people you will ask to help you?**

_____
_____
_____
_____
_____
_____
_____

**Specific Action Steps:** What steps need to be taken to get you to your goal?

_____
_____
_____
_____
_____
_____
_____

# WINNER OR WHINER ... YOUR CHOICE!

▼

**"You can't be a winner if you're a whiner...wiener."** - **Jeffrey Gitomer**

Our time begins at birth and ends at death. For most of us that is about 28,105 days. When you look at from this perspective, it is a little easier to see how precious our time is. We all intellectually know that time cannot be stored up like treasures, yet how does that translate into our daily routines and habits?

Once a day passes it is gone forever. Every morning it credits you with 86,400 seconds and each night writes off as lost whatever you have failed to invest to good purpose. So, the clock is running and to realize it's value, reflect on this commonly used exercise I found on Pinterest. It has been published and spoken by so many:

To realize the value of ONE YEAR, ask a student who failed a grade.

To realize the value of ONE MONTH, ask a soldier whose overseas assignment is nearly over.

To realize the value of ONE WEEK, ask a coach of a football team.

To realize the value of ONE HOUR, ask a personal trainer what is possible.

To realize the value of ONE MINUTE, ask a person who missed the door closing at the airport.

To realize the value of ONE SECOND, ask a person who just avoided an accident.

To realize the value of ONE MILLISECOND, ask the athlete who won a medal in the Olympics.

The point being time waits for no one. And you can choose during the time you have been given to be a winner or a whiner. Said another way, you can have results, or you can have excuses why you do not have what you want.

What is the difference – winner or whiner, results or excuses?

In an earlier chapter you read about the obstacles Benjamin Franklin, Walt Disney, Oprah Winfrey and others have overcome. What's the conclusion? It is simply a mindset.

I was thinking about my first Spartan race, and I did not know what to expect. I learned quickly, the course designers pride themselves in stacking obstacles that test similar muscle groups to expose and exploit your weaknesses. I could be a winner or a whiner. I could get resourceful or blame resources. A good example is the elevation drop at the Spartan Beast in Big Bear, California. One of the highest percent of "did not finish" events of the year. The elevation drop was so severe at times if you ran chest-on downhill you would quickly land on your face! I could stop and whine about the course, or I could get resourceful. Modifying with a zig-zag pattern was the perfect game day modification. The perfect workaround to keep moving forward.

You do not have to run a Spartan race to realize life presents challenges every day. There are all kinds of things you can do to stay in inspired action.

The difference between a winner and a whiner, between results and excuses is getting creative with workarounds. The difference between getting caught up in the weeds – not seeing the workaround - and stepping back and looking at the bigger picture can be summarized in these 5 steps:

**Allocate Time** – sounds obvious yet if it is not in the calendar it does not exist.

**Find A Partner** – two heads are better than one.

**Remove Assumptions** – for each assumption you have, what would happen if you remove it?

**Chunk It Down** – unpack things into smaller bite size deliverables

**Immediate Next Steps** – identify and act on the immediate next steps.

When you find yourself up against an obstacle, are you a whiner or a winner? The characteristics of a whiner vs. a winner:

## Whiners

Whiners only work hard when they "feel" like it. Whiners wait for things to happen. Whiners continually point out what is wrong where they work and with whom they work with.

Whiners have a scarcity mentality. Anytime someone gets something like a "big sale", a bonus, a new piece of equipment they feel that there is that much less for them.

Whiners blame things beyond their control and never take responsibility for what they can control.

Whiners bring their problems to work and wear them on their sleeve.

Whiners use rejection as an excuse to quit.

Whiners do the bare minimum yet expect the most in return.

Whiners have the "disease of me". They are addicted to their own agenda and out for themselves.

Whiners need pep talks. They require high maintenance and attention to continually repair their attitude and outlook.

**Winners**
Winners work hard every day, without letting up... regardless of how they "feel."

Winners make things happen.

Winners can point out what is wrong, yet they have solutions on how to fix it.

Winners have an abundance mentality. They know that there is plenty to go around for everyone who works hard and does their job.

Winners focus strictly on what they can control and do their best to control those areas well. If those areas under perform, they blame no one but themselves.

Winners have problems. The difference is they leave them at home. They do not do or say anything that would distract or bring down another team member, and they stay away from those who do.

Winners use rejection as validation that they are doing something, knowing that it will bring them closer to where they want to be.

Winners give more than they have to and expect nothing more in return, although they often get it.

Winners are team players, often ignoring what is best for them for the good of the team.

Winners give pep talks. They not only cross the finish line, they are intent on bringing others across with them.

During my climb of Mount Kilimanjaro, the day and night of the ascent was one of the hardest days of my life. You start the ascent just before midnight, so you and your team can arrive at the Summit in time for Sunrise. Then you descend, take a quick rest and hike back down to the next camp site.

This was 15 hours or brutal work. That night I had serious doubts if I could finish and hike out the rest of the way. I was nearly in whiner mode. Yet, I chose to step back and reflect on the reasons I was there; I spoke to a close friend that was climbing with me; I removed the assumptions I had about hiking out the next day and broke my next steps down into small action items. I got resourceful in terms of my recovery and the practical steps I could take to recover in time for the next day's work. And I am so glad I did, as the next day's hike out was actually one of my favorite days of the entire climb. If I had listened to my inner "whiner" I would have missed the most amazing portion of the entire trip.

So, which do you prefer: Results or excuses? Whiner or winner?

Excuses are like noses. We have all got one and they smell. Are you going to continue to settle for safe or make One Helluva Move? Some practical steps to take "One Helluva Move" this week:

**For Yourself:**

Review the list of "Whiner" characteristics, do you have any?

_____
_____
_____
_____

What actions can you take to switch any whiner characteristics to winning characteristics?

_____
_____
_____
_____

Review the list of winning characteristics, what are your strongest areas?

_____
_____
_____
_____

What actions cab you take to make your winner characteristics even stronger?

_____
_____
_____
_____

Who will help you maintain accountability to the above?

_____
_____
_____
_____

**For Building Your Team:**

Have each Team Member review the list of "Whiner" characteristics, do they have any?

_____
_____
_____
_____

What actions can they take to switch any whiner characteristics to winning characteristics?

_____
_____
_____
_____

Review the list of "Winning" characteristics, what are the strongest areas?

_____
_____
_____
_____

What actions can they take to make the winner characteristics even stronger?

_____
_____
_____
_____

Who will help you maintain accountability to the above?

_____
_____
_____
_____

# ADDICTED TO ADDICTIONS

**"At the end, someone or something always gives up. It is either you give up and quit or the obstacle or failure gives up and makes way for your success to come through." -** Idowu Koyenikan

Every year since 1987, the Conference Board has conducted a job satisfaction survey. Nearly three decades ago, 61.1% of workers said they liked their jobs. That number has slid over time, reaching an all-time low in 2010 when only 42.6% of workers said they were satisfied in their jobs.

Are you one of them?

If so maybe you are caught up in the drama triangle. The drama triangle is a social model that was conceived by Stephen Karpman. Karpman models the connection between personal responsibility and power in conflicts, and the destructive and shifting roles people play. It can be summarized like this:

**The Victim:** The Victim's stance is "Poor me!" The Victim feels victimized, oppressed, helpless, hopeless, powerless, ashamed, and seems unable to make decisions, solve problems, take pleasure in life, or achieve insight. The Victim, if not being persecuted, will seek out a Persecutor and also a Rescuer who will save the day but also perpetuate the Victim's negative feelings.

**The Rescuer:** The rescuer's line is "Let me help you." A classic enabler, the Rescuer feels guilty if they do not go to the rescue. Yet they fail to see this behavior has negative effects: It keeps the Victim dependent and gives the Victim permission to fail. The rewards derived from this rescue role are that the focus is taken off of the rescuer. When they focus their energy on someone else, it enables them to ignore their own anxiety and issues. This rescue role is also very pivotal because their actual primary interest is really an avoidance of their own problems disguised as concern for the victim's needs.

**The Persecutor:** Is "the Villian." The Persecutor insists, "It is all your fault." The Persecutor is controlling, blaming, critical, oppressive, angry, authoritative, rigid, and superior.

So, here is the question, what role do you play? Which of the labels do you identify with the most?

Do you sometimes tend to complain or act helpless (victim)?

Do you find yourself blaming other people (persecutor)?

Are you the one that enables a problem behavior to continue (the rescuer)?

Now that you have selected a primary role, do you want to approach things differently? If yes, once you are aware of your part, do not do the same thing you have always done, change it up. Here is a model:

**Victims:** Choose not to outsource your self-esteem by seeking validation from other people. Instead, strengthen your decision-making skills and try acting before you feel ready.

**Rescuers:** Pay special attention to what drains your energy, like people or specific activities. To curb people- pleasing, develop firm boundaries. Start to say "no" more than you say "yes."

**Persecutors:** Replace accusatory, sweeping statements like "You always forget to call!" with "I" statements. For example, "When I didn't hear from you, I felt worried." With careful choices we can all replace the drama triangle with the winner's triangle: compassion, listening, and assertiveness.

And the winner is YOU! Let's pause and reflect...

What primary role do you play in the Drama Triangle?

What steps can you take now to move in a new direction?

Who can hold you accountable to this commitment?

**"May your choices reflect your hopes, not your fears."**

Moving on... have you ever wondered, why is it that some people live their lives full of love, abundance and purpose, while others live in a state of fear, lack and indecision?

Napoleon Hill in his book "Think and Grow Rich" outlined a formula for happiness and success this way:

First, have a definite, clear, practical idea, goal or objective.

Second, attain it by whatever means available, whether wisdom, money, materials, or methods.

Third, adjust all your means to that end.

This is as my friend Tom Ferry calls it a "life by design."

Tom explains that people living by design live by a different set of rules. They know a challenge is just temporary, their problems are assets and the past is exactly where it belongs... in the past. They are not victims; they are victors. They are willing to jump through hoops to live the life they dream of. During my trip to climb Mount Kilimanjaro, I have met people who do not have two nickels to rub together, as well as extremely rich people that both fall into this category. Living by design I have learned is not about how much money you have, it is a mindset.

So, what gets in the way?

**THE FOUR ADDICTIONS:**

My friend Tom Ferry, discovered and wrote about four addictions that destroy more dreams, more hopes and more lives than alcohol, drugs, food, gambling or sex combined. What you and I typically think of addictions are really the effects brought on by four much larger causes that are the root cause. Here is what Tom wrote:

**The Addiction to opinions of other people.** Some people are addicted to what others think about us and how others' views of the world affect us.

**The Addiction to drama.** Some people are drawn to and consumed by any event or situation that occupies their thoughts and fills their mind with negativity, which often brings attention to them in unproductive ways.

**The Addiction to the past.** These people have an unhealthy attachment to events or situations that have occurred in the past. They are stuck in how things used to be.

**The Addiction to worry.** This addiction is comprised of all the negative and self-defeating thoughts that make us anxious, disturbed, upset and stressed, that hold us back in life. Of which, most or all never come true.

Getting off the drama triangle and walking away from the four addictions is not something we do once and for all. All of us get on and off all the time. Understanding our behaviors and the triggers begins to help us map a course out. It is a process. The beginning of any recovery is acknowledging that there is a problem and that there is help outside oneself, and the willingness to utilize it.

Excuses are like noses. We have all got one and they smell.

Are you going to continue to settle for safe or make One Helluva Move? Some practical steps to make "One Helluva Move" this week:

**For Yourself:**

Which of the four addictions can you relate to?

_____

What's one action you can take this week to reframe that addiction?

_____

Who can hold you accountable?

_____

**For Building Your Team:**

Do members of your team play the drama triangle?

If yes, which team members play which roles?

Team Member: _____ Triangle Role: _____
Team Member: _____ Triangle Role: _____
Team Member: _____ Triangle Role: _____
Team Member: _____ Triangle Role: _____


Do any team members play the winners triangle?
Team Member: _____ Triangle Role: _____
Team Member: _____ Triangle Role: _____

For those in drama, what coaching, and training can you encourage to make it better?

For those in the winning triangle, how can you celebrate and encourage?

As I write this near the Dallas Cowboys practice facility... consider this, from Tom Landry:

"A coach is someone who tells you what you do not want to hear, who has you see what you do not want to see, so you can be who you have always known you could be."
And you cannot do that by avoiding the tough conversations with yourself or others.

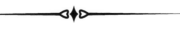

# YOUR ZONE OF GENIUS

**"If you do what you love, you'll never work a day in your life."** – Marc Anthony

Question... What do you most love to do? Those things you love so much you can do it for long stretches of time without getting tired or bored. Have you ever noticed there are moments in our lives when we feel as if we are doing exactly what we were born to do? Our work feels like a privilege and everything we are doing feels like a gift to the world. In these moments we are in what author Gay Hendricks refers to as our personal zone of genius.

You know I have always wondered why games, sports and activities outside work generate so much drive and happiness for people. Guys I have known will spend more time learning baseball stats than work stats. Why is that? It seems simply their work is outside their zone of genius.

Bad news for me. Between being an average student in high school to nearly getting kicked out of college and getting fired by my first customer, the idea that I had any sort of genius sounded like a weird dream. Yet I quickly learned - what I lacked in being a perfect student, lacked in who I knew – was that persistence and determination became my competitive weapon. And I learned a 6-step process to keep me in the zone more and out of my head less.

Think about it for a moment - over the course of your life our social programming driven by the beliefs, opinions, judgements and criticisms of others - it is very possible that you do not believe in your own zone of genius.

I am here to say, **do not believe it!**

Right now, at this very moment – regardless of your past – you have unlimited potential to unlock your zone of genius. I have had a lot of assignments in my career from government, corporate America and small business. From those experiences, I do not think I will ever spend 100% of my time in my zone of genius, yet I love it when I do. My experience and working with hundreds of successful people around the globe, has taught me that there are many activities I need to do that are not in my genius zone but allow me to enjoy freedom when I am in my zone of genius. There is freedom in that thought. It is the price to be paid for freedom.

CrisMarie Campbell and Susan Clarke, Coaches, Business Consultants, Speakers and Authors of The Beauty of Conflict recommend taking an honest look at how you are spending your time through the Four Zone Model:

| Zone of Excellence | Zone of Genius |
|---|---|
| You are very good at these things. They even bring you success, but they don't make your heart sing. | You absolutely love doing these & you're phenomenal at them. These activities give you the highest ratio of abundance and satisfaction to the amount of time spent. |
| **Zone of Incompetence** | **Zone of Incompetence** |
| You don't do these things well. You may not even like doing them and are best reassigned or delegated. | You can do things, but may not like doing them much and could be done better by someone else. |

How do I apply this four-zone model? Draw out the four quadrants and map out your current activities. It does not matter if you are leading a team, running a business or running the home – or in some cases all three! After tracking where you are currently spending the majority of your time, you can decide if that is where you want to stay.

Where are you spending the most of your time?

The good news? There is a way out and way to spend more time in your zone of genius. Here is a 6-step model to consider:

**First, Set Aside Time for Reflection Each Day**
What is really important here? How am I using my gifts? What is my genius and how can I bring it forth to bare on my family and my culture and my business? Those genius questions are things that we need to cultivate in ourselves almost as a matter of discipline.—Gay Hendricks

**Second, Always Be Testing and Collecting Data**
If we were not willing to experiment, we would never find out what works and what does not. Effective experimentation requires you to focus on the process and

not the prize and great ideas require a willingness to be wrong. What are your testing?

### Third, Embrace Non-Linear Thinking
In his book Humans Are Underrated: What High Achievers Know That Brilliant Machines Never Will, Geoff Colvin outlines that robots will almost definitely be better than humans are at number crunching and linear processes. Basically, he states humans are really good at being human, we have just lost the time and inclination to do that. As we seek to be relevant in a world that is being taken over by robots, mastering non-linear thinking and creativity becomes critical.

Geoff outlines humans greatest advantage lies in empathy, creativity, social sensitivity, storytelling, humor, building relationships, and expressing ourselves with greater power than logic can ever achieve. This in his view is how we create durable value that is not easily replicated by technology—because we are hardwired to want this things from humans.

### Fourth, Become A Producer
Producers have a bias towards action, which shows itself in the propensity to make ideas real and operational, so they can be tested with actual customers. — John Sviokla and Mitch Cohen, The Self-Made Billionaire Effect. When you are in action mistakes can happen yet so can brilliance. Would you rather take the chance to keep getting ready to get ready?

### Fifth, Apply The Four-Zone Model Monthly
Like any other habit, what you measure improves. What you measure and have an accountability partner the improvement is exponential! Apply the four-zone model monthly at minimum or anytime you are feeling out of sorts.

**Sixth, Delegate, Automate or Eliminate**

I have seen too many entrepreneurs follow this idea like it is some kind of commandment: "If you want something done right, you have to do it yourself." Can you relate? Imagine if you could automate or eliminate most of the tasks you disliked (booking appointments, marketing yourself, writing blog posts), thus leaving you more time to do what you love and find important. What would happen to your personal productivity and your life satisfaction? The key to delegation... they will not do it like you. Automation, explore tools like "If this than that." IFTTT is the free way to get all your apps and devices talking to each other. Not everything on the internet plays nice, so IFTTT is on a mission to build a more connected world. Let it go and thrive in the genius zone.

The greatest work of your life is inside each of us. Give it the fertile soil - the personal habits and disciplines - it needs to see the light of day. Plant the seeds each day and you will open yourself up to an infinite set of possibilities.

What is possible for you?

**Dissatisfaction is a symptom of high performers!**

John Milton, said it well: "The mind is its own place, and in itself can make a heaven of hell, or a hell of heaven."

Our mind is the most powerful tool we have at our disposal. It can create beautiful things, spread joy, and change the world. But it can also create much suffering in our own life. It is up to us to decide how we use it.

While writing this book I made One Helluva Move from Southern California to the great state of Texas with clear goals and a bright future. Yet something was off. I could not put my finger on it, but deep down I knew I was not truly happy. Every day, I tried to put on a happy face, both online and offline, and convince myself that everything was OK. But inside, I kept wondering what the hell was wrong with me. This was exceptionally challenging because I am a coach, I have developed a brand as the guy that inspires, the guy who is always happy, upbeat, and loving life. But all of a sudden, I was not truly that guy. I felt out of integrity to my values and trapped.

Here is what I discovered, I had not been living in the "here and now". I had been so busy thinking about the past, the future, and worrying about the present, that I was not fully appreciating what was in front of me. I was letting my mind run all sorts of deflating patterns. I was allowing my self talk to reminisce about how good things were before... in a sense making me feel like the best years of my life were behind me. I would allow my mind to ponder on why the present was so challenging... making me wish things were easier while wondering why I was not reaching my goals faster. I would let myself worry about the uncertainty of living in a new city and second guessing my decision of moving there, and then allowing myself to stress about it. In short, I was letting my mind control me and I was sabotaging my own happiness.

You see, I have observed and learned first-hand that dissatisfaction is a symptom of top performers. We set such high expectations of ourselves.

Can you relate?

For me, I fell into the trap I knew so well. Fortunately, because it is not my first rodeo, and I am so aware of the path out, turning this around was easier.

So, if you are in a funk or just looking to raise the level of satisfaction in your life, here is what I have learned along the way.

**First, take responsibility.**
Happiness is a choice. Here is what I have discovered: if you are unhappy right now, it is because of the things you choose to think about and, you have the power to change that instantly.

**Second, be present in the here and now.**
Whenever we are leaving behind a great chapter of our life, whether it's a past job, a past relationship, or a bucket list adventure that is over, we have a tendency to hang on to it. We keep thinking about it, wishing we could go back. In most cases this only creates sufferance. The past is gone. Right now is all we have got. On the opposite side of that fence, when we worry about the future. That is another choice we are making. The reality is that the only thing within our control is what we are doing right now. Anything else is just wasted emotional energy.

**Third, surrender to what is and declare it perfect.**
Whenever I have argued with reality, I have always lost! I have learned, whenever I am in a sub-optimal situation, whether it is being stuck in traffic, or going through a challenging period in life or at work, getting upset about it serves no purpose. It is like trying to argue with reality, with what already is. Yet we do it all the time. Does this sound familiar?

Why does this always happen to ME!
What does it have to be like THAT?
My life was easier WHEN...!

Eckhart Tolle wrote: "The primary cause of unhappiness is never the situation but your thoughts about it. It is the label we put on them that makes them positive or negative." I have stated this concept another way. The three decisions we all control:

What we FOCUS on
The meaning in ATTACH to things, and What we do despite the obstacles we face

**Fourth, create more no mind moments**
Research shows we have between 50,000 and 70,000 thoughts per day. This means between 35 and 48 thoughts per minute per person! How exhausting and how much of that is unnecessary? Without a disciplined approach, and a well-developed mental toughness, all this constant mental traffic can prevent us from seeing clearly, listening deeply, and feeling our well of being. For me it is super hard to create those quiet moments... so I turn to prayer and exercise like yoga, a bike ride, a run, a walk-in nature or a group workout with no expectations.

**Fifth serve others**
Gandhi said it best, "the best way to find yourself is to lose yourself in the service of others."

I learned the hard way, when going through a tough time, it is easy to isolate yourself, but it is only going to make things worse. When I purposely seek the presence of people I love, people who inspire me. And then go a step further: do my best to make them happy. Smile, ask how they are doing, and help them with their challenges. I have found the more I focus on their happiness, the more mine arrives. For me this comes to me by volunteering – at church, at the homeless shelter or a community event.

Excuses are like noses. We have all got one and they smell. Are you going to continue to settle for safe or make One Helluva Move? Some practical steps to make "One Helluva Move" this week:

**For Yourself:**

What zone are you spending 80% of your time in?

_____
_____
_____

What can you delegate and let go of this week?

_____
_____
_____

Which 6-step model can you best benefit from in the next 30 days? (the Zone of Genius Model or the Happiness Model)

_____
_____
_____

Who can hold you accountable?

_____
_____
_____

**For Building Your Team:**

For each of your team members, where are they spending their time, in which zone?

_____
_____
_____

How can you help your team members off-load tasks that are not their highest and best use?

_____
_____
_____

Who can take on those tasks?

_____
_____
_____

What will happen for them and the business when you move forward with this new model?

_____
_____
_____

# PEOPLE MATTER, YOUR LOGO IS SECONDARY

---

**"Your personal brand is what people say about you when you are not in the room – remember that. And more importantly, let's discover why!"** - Chris Drucker

People matter, and your logo is secondary... wow that is going turn some heads. As this type of unconventional thinking is counter intuitive to what many of you are thinking right now. Let me explain.

Coming from a fairly extensive consumer package goods experience I can state clearly that selling and marketing a product is totally different than selling a professional service. I see so many agents in my field start – or stop an existing business – and spend an inordinate amount of time on what their logo will look like while ignoring all the relationships around them! They confused a logo for what their brand really stands for.

My friend, CEO & Founder of JP & Associates REALTORS®, JP Picininni wrote about it, this way. "Coming out of engineering I knew if I created and followed a formula, my BRAND would be created, and success would flow. And it did, following my 7 S formula I created a brand name for myself and became the #1 producer in my office. Later in my career, I had the skills, desire and drive to create my own real estate brokerage. In the last 6 years – following the 7 S formula - that brand made One Helluva Move from being a dream to now the 88th largest real estate brokerage firm in America!"

So, what is this formula that created such a strong brand?

It is the 7 S's:

Suit Up
Show Up
Specialize
Solicit daily
Spend wisely
Set Specific Goals
Service (give back and contribute)

You see JP spent more of his time delivering on his promises; creating relationships and being known for something than he did on his logo. The logo really did not matter too much. And you can do the same. Now I am not suggesting that a logo and a consistent theme are not an important element of your image... I am suggesting that it is just ONE element. Do not spend a career on it because at the end of the day, as JP stated the 7 S's become what you are known for and your TRUE brand.

As I write this, in my industry the National Association of Realtors® just released a new logo. I'm sure a big-name firm was paid lots of money. Unfortunately, it has become a social media nightmare and a distraction for the brand. All the leaders in the industry and agents across the fruited plain are buzzing about it. Could any of that energy be redirected to building relationships and fulfilling promises? I think so.

At the end of day REALTORS® stand for the code of ethics and all that that means is the promises we make and keep, the commitments we follow through on and the service we deliver whereby the consumer is surprised and delighted. NAR's CEO Bob Goldberg said it this way: "As we tried to reimagine our REALTOR® R, we thought about the people behind the brand—the human beings who are making the real estate transaction happen. Consumers trust our members and our brand represents trust. We don't ever want to lose sight of the fact that the human factor makes the brand what it is."

It was a Sunday afternoon, and I just wanted to get out and about, so I stopped by my favorite Starbucks location, I placed my order sat down and I notice some sophisticated coffee equipment in front of me. I started the ask the barista a few questions. It turns out I was sitting in front of a syphon brewing station. The barista started to explain how it worked and low and behold other customers gathered around to hear about it. Then one of the customers ordered one... and the barista went into action explaining the entire process, how it came about and basically the art and science of syphon brewing. It was awesome, entertaining and such a surprise and delight. The Starbucks brand moved up several notches in my world. It had nothing to do with a logo. I just stopped in for a cup of coffee!

So how do we go about building a brand for ourselves.

First, we need research the target audience and the competition.

Second, we need to pick a focus and a personality in approaching the marketplace.

Third, we have to be clear on the problem we solve and our unique selling proposition.

Forth, design the systems, structure and process to deliver on your promise.

Fifth, create the design elements, look and feel that best represents your offering.

It seems so many people I begin to work with start backwards with step 5 and invest so much time and treasure they end up skipping steps 1 to 4.

Picking and understanding a target market. Targeting a specific market does not mean that you are excluding people who do not fit your criteria. Rather, target marketing allows you to focus your marketing dollars and brand message on a specific market that is more likely to buy from you than other markets. This is a much more affordable, efficient, and effective way to reach potential clients and generate business. With a clearly defined target audience, it is much easier to determine where and how to market your services. Of course, you will have a false start if you do not include a deep look the current competition and how you can differentiate yourself. (Quicker, faster, easier, cheaper, full service, etc.)

Pick a focus and a personality. We have seen that specialist thrive and generalist struggle. If you try to be all things to all people you automatically reduce you chance of success. So, what is your focus – in residential real estate that could be the hyper local expert in a specific neighborhood. In commercial real estate that could be industrial, multi-family or retail. And in what personality will you approach the market? Some have success approaching the market as the social butterfly and the community connector. Others have success being the analytical market trends and insight expert. Others see success by becoming the HUB of information for a hyper local area.

What is the problem you solve in the marketplace? Your unique selling proposition might go like this.

We offer (product or service) to (target market) by (value proposition).

Unlike (the alternatives) we (key differentiator).

Example: "We offer full service, one stop shopping for home sellers in the Main Street Community by dramatically reducing the stress and hassle of selling your home and moving. Unlike others, we have a complete concierge service that becomes your hub central during the selling and moving process. And at the end of our work together we donate a portion of our proceeds to our local school teachers."

Your business operating system (BOS). Now none of this means anything without the structure, systems and process to back it up. Great agents and teams create and reinforce a rigorous discipline about the little things that affect their customers. They instill a discipline in their business operating systems and reinforce discipline at a personal level. Personal and organizational discipline help breathe life into your BOS and enable you to sustain it over time, making it the way you do business rather than just a set of hollow procedures. A description of the five components is presented in priority order:

Processes
Systems
Roles
Skills
Structure

Winston Churchill said, "For the first 25 years of my life I wanted freedom. For the next 25 years I wanted order. For the next 25 years I realized that order is freedom". Your business operating system will provide you and your business the order and freedom to work on your business rather than in it.

You will need a mentor, a coach someone who has gone before you and willing to share. Invest in this as it is the #1 item all top team leaders tell me: "I wish I would have asked for help or hired a coach sooner!"

Finally, the logo and the creative elements to pull the look and feel that represents the promise. Unless your trained in this area keep it simple: hire an expert in your local community or on FIVERR. Keep it simple, clean and straight forward because at the end of the day for most of us in the service business, people matter, and your logo is secondary.

Like my Starbucks story where the brand promises were delivered by a barista that decided to surprise and delight.

Excuses are like noses. We have all got one and they smell. Are you going to continue to settle for safe or make One Helluva Move? Some practical steps to make "One Helluva Move" this week:

For Yourself:
What is your brand... what do you stand for?

_____

How can you differentiate yourself?

_____

How can you surprise and delight buyers or sellers this week? _____

How often do your survey your clients, prospects and vendors? What did you learn? _____

Who can hold you accountable to the above?

_____

_____

Is your personal operating system defined? (think of your POS like your BOS)

_____

_____

**For Building Your Team:**

What are each of your team members known for?

_____

_____

Any adjustments need to be made?

_____

_____

Do you have standards they must meet with each client?

_____

_____

How often do your survey your clients, prospects and vendors? What did you learn?

_____

_____

How often do you practice dialogs (buyer presentation, seller presentation, common objections) as a team?

_____

_____

Is your business operating system (BOS) defined?

_____

_____

# GETTING READY TO GET READY

**"Begin doing what you want to do now. We are not living in eternity. We have only this moment, sparkling like a star in our hand—and melting like a snowflake."** - Francis Bacon

The conclusion... I have interviewed several leading coaches and counselors and they all agree, the root cause of the why people procrastinate comes from self-limiting beliefs. When these limiting thoughts go unchecked, they cause you to make excuses for why a project, a task or an activity cannot be completed. When you challenge these excuses, yo will see that most if not all of them are caused by hidden fears or destructive habit patterns. So, what is the solution?

Here is what I know, until you get into some type of positive action your brain wont process what is required. So, what stops us from taking action, from moving forward right now?

1. Avoidance & Deflection (Busy work because it is easier and provides a sense of completion)
2. Unclear on how to get started
3. Too easily distracted
4. Lack of skill
5. Lack of interest
6. Lack of motivation
7. Fear of failure
8. Fear of success
9. Resistance
10. Perfectionism

Many of these excuses can be tied to a fixed mindset. You will know you have a fixed mindset if you believe that your personal qualities are fixed traits and cannot change. If you

document your intelligence and talents rather than working to develop and improve them. If you believe that talent alone leads to success, and effort is not required.

Alternatively, if you have growth mindset, you will have an underlying belief that your learning and intelligence can grow with time and experience. You believe you and others can get smarter, you realize that your effort has an effect on success, so you are willing to put in extra time, leading to higher achievement.

Let's cover perfectionism and resistance in a little more detail.

## Challenge: Perfectionism

Perhaps you are worried you might make a mistake, expose a weakness or be subjected to reticule. The fear of making mistakes is a real, and it causes many people to put off some of their important obligations for another day. While some may think that being a perfectionist is a positive trait, it is actually quite detrimental. It is a dangerous mix of anti-productive habits and attitudes that discourage progression. Although often misunderstood as having high standards, perfectionism limits the definition of success to an unrealistic standard. This standard will never be achieved, so why try?

## Solution: Perfectionism

Surrender. When we surrender to the moment, to change, to imperfection, we allow excellence to grow. Excellence is that drive toward raising ourselves up to our own highest and best use and allowing our unique talents and personalities to come out. Excellence, unlike perfectionism, is about pushing ourselves to act, think, relate, and create at the highest level. Perfectionism on the other hand, is about trying to control the outcome in order to receive typically approval or acceptance. Its fear based.

66

Surrendering is about accepting where we are at in any moment, knowing that we are a work in progress and accepting some mistakes along the way. Think like a scientist trying to prove or disprove a hypothesis. It is a growth mindset orientation.

## Challenge: Resistance

Some of us just appear to be not that interested in change, in self-improvement, in learning or getting along with others. Why? A few theories to consider:

**Poor self-image:** If you do not think you can complete a project or a task you are already doomed. These are folks who, at the first hint of trouble, abandon even fledgling efforts. Any negative feedback just confirms what they already believe: they are not smart or good enough; they will never be able to figure it out. Counselors and psychologists agree, developing a strong self-image regarding oneself as someone able to acquire new skills, knowledge, behaviors, and insights—is a crucial psychological underpinning to avoiding resistance.

**Not connecting the dots:** if you cannot connect the task, project or activity to some relevant bigger picture, resistance naturally occurs.

**Fear of the unknown:** This type of resistance occurs mainly when change is implemented without warning the affected stakeholders before the change occurs. When change (especially what is perceived as negative change) is pushed onto people without giving them adequate warning and without helping them through the process of understanding what the change will include and how their jobs/work will be affected, it can cause people to push back against the change due to their fear of the unknown.

**Inappropriate level of activity:** when the level of activity is too fast, too intense the frustrations turns to resistance.

Heaping too much change over a short period of time can cause resistance. If change is not implemented at the right time or with the right level of tact or empathy, it usually will not work.

**Mistrust:** Trust is everything. In the absence of trust there is only fear.

### Solution: Resistance

**Become more aware:** The problem usually is not that we do not think about resistance. We simply do not understand it. We think, "Oh, I better straighten out my desk ... or get my to-do lists in order" or we get distracted by something on the web, or we feel that we have to check our email, or we are just going to watch this one TV show, or any of a limitless amount of distractions. Combat this by realizing that you are facing resistance. Once you become aware of it, you can fight it, and beat it. It can be difficult to become more aware, but the key is to focus on it for a couple of days. Print out the words "Defeat Resistance" and put it somewhere visible as you work. That will help remind you to be aware of resistance.

**Be very clear, and focused:** Before you start the day, be very clear about what you want to accomplish. You will not be able to finish 5 major projects, but you can finish one important project, or at least move it along to a certain point. Set the three most important outcomes you want to accomplish on this day. Once you have those things defined, focus on them to the exclusion of all else. Do them first. Focus, finish, then move on to the smaller tasks you need to complete today. If you find yourself being lured to do something that's not on that short list of three things, bring yourself back and focus.

**Just start:** At the end of the day, all the tips in the world will not make as much a difference as this simple instruction. Just sit down and start. Feel any resistance to doing just that? There is no better way to overcome it than to just start. Reading more about resistance will not help. Working on your to-do lists will not help. Only doing actually helps and the only way to do something is to just start.

So how do you start, when you feel resistance? You just start. Feeling the need to do something else? Stop yourself from getting distracted. Remind yourself what you need to be doing, and why. Sit down and the set time and place. And just start.

Your mind is an amazing machine. It gives you the power to create anything from your imagination. However, it can also limit your ability to get things done. Nobody is immune to making procrastination excuses. No matter how successful you are, at some point you will come up with a reason to not take action on a project. That is why it is important to form habits that specifically prevent and overcome the excuses. o quickly sweep the reasons for procrastination right out the door. Once you understand the why of procrastination it is easier to move into action.

The key to beating procrastination is to find out what your specific reasons are for doing so, and then addressing them at their root cause. Charles Duhigg, explained it best in his book The Power of Habit: Why We Do What We Do In Life and Business Duhigg states, the Habit loop is a neurological pattern that governs any habit. It consists of three elements: a cue, a routine, and a reward. Understanding these components can help in understanding how to change bad habits or form good ones. The habit loop is always started with a cue, a trigger that transfers your brain into a mode that automatically determines which habit to use. The heart of the habit is a mental, emotional, or physical routine. Finally, there is a reward, which helps your brain determine if this particular loop is worth remembering for the future.

In an article in The New York Times, Duhigg notes, "The cue and reward become neurologically intertwined until a sense of craving emerges." Craving drives all habits and is essential to starting a new habit or destroying an old one." Find the "trigger or the cue" name it and claim and that is the first step. The trick that I have found is creating or substituting new triggers or cues, new routines and new rewards.

Excuses are like noses. We have all got one and they smell. Are you going to continue to settle for safe or make One Helluva Move? Some practical steps to make "One Helluva Move" this week:

**For Yourself:**
Think about the concept of putting things off, procrastinating or getting ready to get ready as a sports play. What plays are you running that do not serve you well? In sports, we would create a new play, a new approach to the game.

Do you have a FIXED or a GROWTH mindset?

_____

_____

How does your current mindset serve you?

_____

_____

Of the 10 excuses to put things off, which is your dominate behavior? _____

What instant "reward" do you get by procrastinating?

_____

_____

Can you identify the trigger or the cue that drives the behavior? _____

When triggered, can you identify a new routine, a new behavior you can start instead?

_____

_____

Can you create a new "reward" for when you run this new "play." _____

Who can you share this with and ask them to be an accountability partner?

_____

_____

**For Building Your Team:**
Think about the concept of putting things off, procrastinating or getting ready to get ready as a sports play. What plays are you running that don't serve you well? In sports, we would create a new play, a new approach to the game.

For each team member, do they have a FIXED or a GROWTH mindset?

_____

_____

How does that mindset serve them in the workplace?

_____

_____

As a team go through the individual exercise above. Plus, as a team, discuss the most common reasons for resistance and which ones impact your team.

Transparency rules in this exercise... so resistance is futile!

Discuss accountability to the changes you've agreed to make.

# FINAL THOUGHTS

Albert Einstein once said, **"Never seek to become a person of success. Seek to become a person of value. Then the success will come."**

When I was making some difficult decisions to change things up in my own life several years ago, my friend and mentor Tom Ferry shared some advice he learned from the great Mike Vance. He asked me five thought-provoking and life-altering questions to help me envision and then plan out the path I should take.

Why are you here — what is your purpose?

_____

_____

How do you want to show up for others — what are your values?

_____

_____

What are your God-given talents?

_____

_____

Five years from now, how is the world experiencing you?

_____

_____

Who would you already be if you were already there?

_____

_____

I trust this will help you as you create your life and business by design.

_____

# BONUS SECTION:

# 7 THINGS I WISH MY BROKER HAD TOLD ME

JP Piccinini, CEO and Founder of JP & Associate REALTORS®

Most of you reading this don't know my story. I am immigrant from Italy that came to America – Texas - barely speaking any English and now, the leader of the 88th largest real estate broker in America. Like many of you I came out of corporate America and started my real estate career. When I made that choice living in South Carolina, I did not have an extensive network because I worked 80 hours a week. I wasn't as well connected in the community as others. I was starting a business from scratch and I knew excuses would not create income. So, I took what I knew from engineering – system, structure and process – and applied that to my business. Quickly I became the #1 producing team in my office. Then I took "one helluva a move" from South Carolina back to Texas.

In the last 6 years, my team and I have grown from the trunk of my car to #3 in the DFW marketplace and #88 in the nation. I created JP & Associates REALTORS to provide a solution for top producing agents and teams, I wanted to create a culture of productivity and service, I wanted to help others overcome the 7 things I wish my broker had told me when I started:

What do you need to know as a professional agent in real estate sales?

First, my conclusion... instant success is very rare. I've learned there are simply no shortcuts on the road to success in real estate sales. It takes hard work dedication and what I call the "7 S's" of success:

Suit Up
Show Up
Specialize
Solicit
Spend
Set Goals
Service

Yet I've also learned there are no speed limits either, there is no governor. You can move as fast – or as slow - as you can, and no one is going to stop you. You see I learned in real estate sales that daily success is never owned it's only rented. And in real estate sales, the rent is DUE every day!

Second, don't confuse being an independent contractor with being the CEO of your own business. It's true you are an independent contractor; however, that does not mean you're free to do whatever you please. I wish my broker had told me, being the CEO of your own business... that happens when you unite your talent with your leadership skills. Understanding where you are now; creating an action plan to eliminate gaps; developing systems, structure, and process for your business and having the mental disciplines to win is what separates the rich from the rest.

Third, the job of ALL marketing and social campaigns is to generate appointments that lead to signed contracts, period. When I was selling full time, my sole objective was to participate in activities and marketing that led to signed contracts. Everything else was secondary, delegated or automated. That means assertive networking, self-promotion and relationship building.

Fourth, generalist struggle while specialists thrive. Meaning create a niche for yourself. I see so many of you trying to be all things to all people. "I'll go anywhere!" Really? Why? Because you are so afraid of where the next deal comes from. Develop your brand so you are known for something... "the condo queen," the "luxury home specialist," the "relocating executive expert," the "investment hub for doctors, lawyers and other professionals." Be known for something, not everything. Stay in your lane... if you get a commercial deal refer that to a specialist; you get a short sale lead refer that to an expert; you have lead for farm and ranch refer that to the folks that know "the dirt." Going outside your expertise is the fastest way to disaster in your business.

Fifth, I quickly learned that when I help people achieve their goals it's easier for me to achieve mine. I never approached a potential customer with how much commission I could make. I always served my potential customer with what they needed. Once I understood the importance of allowing people to make their own choices in finding a place to live my business changed. I learned to become the HUB, the local area expert and my brand stood out as the go-to guy.

Sixth, I wish my broker has told me that my colleagues could be both good friends and tough competitors. No one owns the business – not them and not you. It's the only job you wake up each day unemployed. Brining more value than you charge, consistently innovating and being the hyper local expert can be your competitive advantage.

Seventh, I wish I'd known the fact that everything in real estate stays the same, yet everything changes. Typically, in 90-day cycles. Every day you will be presented with challenges and opportunities to stay ahead of technology and the industry. Without a wildly important goal that has meaning to you, a well-defined business plan, a clear target market and a process to test new lead sources each quarter and a method to evaluate it all you'll simply be whipped around by the forces to be vs. building a business by design.

**What to do next?**

At the end of the day, decide what you want; create a compelling reason why you want it; find an accountability partner; stay committed vs just interested; execute your plan with passion; remain flexible yet focused and finally celebrate the small wins along the way. I'd leave you with the exercise, with this action plan for today:

Think about what the next 5 years, the next 10 years look like for you. When you stand there and look back at today, who do YOU NEED TO BE to make that happen? Go BE that person today!

# Bonus 2:

# GRATITUDE & OUTCOMES JOURNAL

Researchers have not only identified significant social, psychological, and physical health benefits that come from giving thanks; they've zeroed in on some concrete practices that help reap those benefits.

The most popular practice is to keep a "gratitude journal." Studies have traced a range of benefits to the simple act of writing down the things for which we're grateful... benefits including better sleep, fewer symptoms of illness, and more joy and happiness.

The basic practice is straightforward and simple. Record the things you've experience in the last 24 hours. The entries are brief— just a single word or a sentence if you choose. They range from the mundane, to the sublime to the timeless.

Emmons, a professor at the University of California, Davis, shared these research-based tips for reaping the greatest psychological rewards from your gratitude journal.

Don't just go through the motions. Research by psychologist Sonja Lyubomirsky suggests that journaling is more effective if you first make the conscious decision to become happier, joyful and more grateful. "Motivation to become happier plays a role in the efficacy of journaling," says Emmons.

Go for depth over breadth. A particular thing for which you're grateful carries more benefits than a superficial list of many things.

Get personal. Focusing on people to whom you are grateful has more of an impact than focusing on things for which you are grateful.

Try subtraction, not just addition. One effective way of stimulating gratitude is to reflect on what your life would be like without certain blessings, rather than just tallying up all those good things.

Savor surprises. Try to record events that were unexpected or surprising, as these tend to elicit stronger levels of gratitude.

There are several APPS out there, Gratitude Journal, Gratitude Dairy. Here's a format I use, experiment with this, one of the APPS or you can create your own... there is no wrong way!

# Gratitude & Outcomes Journal

## Start of Day:

I Am Releasing:

        1. _____

        2. _____

        3. _____

I Am Grateful for:

        1. _____

        2. _____

        3. _____

I Am Grateful for:

        1. _____

        2. _____

        3. _____

Outcomes This Week Outcomes This Month

What Will Make Today Great?

_____
_____
_____
_____
_____

**End of Day**

What Made Today Great?

_____
_____
_____
_____
_____

What Could Be Better Tomorrow?

_____
_____
_____
_____
_____

# BONUS 3:

# DAILY CHECKLIST

Working with startup entrepreneurs, I've learned one thing: most of us can't keep a schedule.

So, while I believe if it's not in your calendar it simply doesn't exist, I know that doesn't work for everyone. I've found a few things that do work. Keeping a daily action checklist is one of them.

A manual checklist like the one in this section works or an APP, like **PRODUCTIVE**; **QUIP**; **CLEAR** and **GOOGLE KEEP** to name a few.

**Benefits:**
Checklists document the daily behaviors required.
Remember process goals and leading indicators?
Checklists help remind you when you get off schedule.
Checklists help you celebrate smaller wins.

There is NO WRONG WAY to keep a checklist, it's finding the one that works for you, so experiment with an APP or a form that this until you find the perfect fit.

Maybe a paper form works best for you, maybe an APP. You decide!

| Daily Checklist | MON | TUE | WED | THU | FRI | SAT | SUN |
|---|---|---|---|---|---|---|---|
| Daily Habits | | | | | | | |
| | | | | | | | |
| | | | | | | | |
| | | | | | | | |
| | | | | | | | |
| Most Important Business Outcomes | | | | | | | |
| | | | | | | | |
| | | | | | | | |
| | | | | | | | |
| | | | | | | | |
| | | | | | | | |
| Most Important Personal Outcomes | | | | | | | |
| | | | | | | | |
| | | | | | | | |
| | | | | | | | |
| | | | | | | | |
| Week In Review | | | | | | | |
| | | | | | | | |
| | | | | | | | |
| | | | | | | | |
| | | | | | | | |

# BONUS 4:

## SUMMARY OF 5 LESSONS LEARNED IN OVER 10,000 HOURS OF 1 ON 1 COACHING SESSIONS

### #1 - The Silent Dream Killer Lesson

Tired of not getting what you want? The 5 words that kill more dreams, more potential, and more happiness than any other 5 words spoken:

**"I don't feel like it."**

How many times have you said, "I don't feel like it?" How many times have you listened to that thought, allowing it to alter the course of your actions? What if you could make a different choice?

### #2 - The GRIT Lesson

If you have not listened to Angela Duckworth's TED talk on GRIT, I'd recommend you do that today!

The theme I run on is: "Results come from an obsession of getting yourself to take action."

Maybe it will help you, as it always helps me when I remember this:

- Grapes must be crushed to make wine
- Diamonds form under pressure
- Olives are pressed to release oil
- Seeds GROW in darkness

So, whenever you feel crushed, pressure, or in the darkness's remember GRIT and remind yourself you are in a powerful place of TRANSFORMATION.

### #3 – The Work Expands To The Time Given Lesson

If you're into productivity, you'll know this proverb as Parkinson's Law. This interesting statement was made by Cyril Northcote Parkinson, the famous British historian, and author.

Parkinson's Law – work expands to fill the time available for its completion – means that if you give yourself a week to complete a two-hour task, then (psychologically speaking) the task will increase in complexity and become more daunting, so as to fill that week. It may not even fill the extra time with more work, but just stress and tension about having to get it done. By assigning the right amount of time to a task, we gain back more time, and the task will reduce complexity to its natural state.

### #4 The Knowledge – Action = 0 Lesson

Knowledge + Action = Winning I've coached a few folks that told me, "I want to produce more... my desire is to be more consistent." Some have been saying this for way too long. Why... fear. Fear keeps our behavior inconsistent with our goals.

Figure out where you want to go, start with the end in mind, and work your way backward to the moment at hand with ACTION.

The error has to do with the difference between **being in motion and taking action**. They sound similar, but they're not the same.

When you're in motion, you're planning and strategizing and learning. Those are all good things, but they **don't produce a result**. Action, on the other hand, is the type of behavior that will **deliver an outcome.**

At the end of the day, the winners are the doers.

### #5 – The Grace Lesson
We are living in unprecedented times. Grace and Grit may go hand in hand together.

Think about it; everyone is NOT like YOU!

Different is not bad; it is just different. A lack of understanding of ourselves and others can lead to real problems such as tension, disappointment, hurt feelings, unmet expectations, and poor communication. As you know, it is hard to work with a problem, especially if you do not understand what is going on inside the mind of another person.

One way to understand what others value is by discovering their BANK code. **BANK Codes** are an easy to use **personality** assessment used to determine your customers' values and what core ideals shape their worldviews. There are four **personality** types in **BANK Codes**: Blueprint, Action, Nurturing, and Knowledge.

This basically means 75% of others are not like YOU and have a different set of key values. Understanding this concept might just be the breakthrough you are looking for.

Grace, to me, is kindness, favor, dignity, and respect. It means being thoughtful and diplomatic, but it doesn't mean being a doormat.

# CONSIDER THIS

Weather you received One Helluva Move as a gift, borrowed it from a friend, or purchased it yourself, we are glad you read it.

We think you will agree Mark has a refreshing voice, an innovative perspective. We hope you will share this book and his thoughts with your co-workers, family and friends. Pay it forward to someone in need.

If you are interested in writing to the author, wish to receive updates, or are interested in coaching with or having Mark speak at your next event please contact us by:

**e-Mail** : coach.mj@icloud.com
or connect via **LinkedIn**

# ABOUT THE AUTHOR

Mark is the host of "Success Superstars" a weekly show that highlights the blueprint of success, the co-founder of CoRecruit and the Chief Executive Officer of JP & Associates REALTORS®, a rapidly growing full-service transaction based real estate brokerage. He has invested nearly 25 years in understanding the inner workings of high performing real estate agents, teams, managers, and leaders in major markets across the world. Mark has served as a business coach, in progressive leadership capacities for the 5th largest US-based real estate brokerage firm; in sales and customer marketing leadership capacities for a major consumer goods company; and served a stint in the US Army. He was later recalled to active duty during the desert storm campaign. Mark is a father of 3, a lifelong learner, Spartan and adventure athlete. He earned his MBA from California State University and a Behavioral Change Certification from the National Association of Sports Medicine. A number of years ago he decided to make "One Helluva Move" and not play it safe, and since then in his spare time he has climbed the world's tallest free-standing mountain - Kilimanjaro; completed the Spartan tri-fecta, the LA Marathon and the world-famous Iowa border to border RABGRAI ride among other crazy adventures.

Made in the USA
Middletown, DE
03 March 2021